The IEA Health and Welfare Unit

Religion in Liberty No. 3

Teaching Right and Wrong:
Have the Churches Failed?

**Rt Rev Michael Adie
Jon Davies
Rabbi Dr Julian Jacobs
Revd John Kennedy
Rt Rev David Konstant
Rev William F. Wallace**

Robert Whelan (Editor)

IEA Health and Welfare Unit
London, 1994

First published November 1994

The IEA Health and Welfare Unit
2 Lord North St
London SW1P 3LB

© The IEA Health and Welfare Unit 1994

ISBN 0-255 36357-5

Typeset by the IEA Health and Welfare Unit
in New Century Schoolbook 10 on 11 point
Printed in Great Britain by
Goron Pro-Print Co. Ltd
Churchill Industrial Estate, Lancing, West Sussex

Contents

Foreword

F.A. Hayek, the leading classical-liberal thinker of the twentieth century, acknowledged the central part played by churches in maintaining the values which underpin liberty. In his last book, *The Fatal Conceit*, he argues that the values, virtues, habits and dispositions essential to a free society, 'are not transmitted automatically'.[1] We must take pains, he says, to pass our values from generation to generation through teaching, historically a task carried out by churches. Hayek had also emphasised the importance of religious movements for freedom during his address to the first meeting of the Mont Pelerin Society in 1947. He went so far as to say that, unless the breach between 'true liberal and religious convictions' could be healed, there was 'no hope for a revival of liberal forces'.[2]

Under the guidance of Robert Whelan, we asked several church leaders to comment on how well their churches were fulfilling their historic task of teaching the virtues that make freedom possible. Their reflections are presented in *Teaching Right and Wrong: Have the Churches Failed?*

David G. Green

Notes

1 Hayek, F.A., *The Fatal Conceit: The Errors of Socialism*, London: Routledge, 1988, p. 136.

2 'Opening address to a conference at Mont Pelerin', in *Studies in Philosophy, Politics and Economics*. London: Routledge & Kegan Paul, 1967, p. 155.

The Authors

Rt Rev Michael Adie has just retired as Bishop of Guildford. He served for five years as Chairman of the Church of England Board of Education. Apart from National Service in the Army, he has spent his entire working life in the ordained ministry in different parts of the country, including London, Sunderland, Sheffield and Lincolnshire.

Jon Davies is a Lecturer at the University of Newcastle upon Tyne, where he is Head of the Religious Studies Department. He was born in 1939 and educated in Kenya and later at Exeter College, Oxford, and Brandeis University, Mass., USA. He is married with three children. He was for nearly twenty years a Labour member of Newcastle upon Tyne City Council. In 1972 he published *The Evangelistic Bureaucrat: a Study of a Planning Exercise in Newcastle upon Tyne* (Tavistock Press). In 1993 he co-edited (with Isabel Wollaston of Birmingham University) *The Sociology of Sacred Texts* and in 1994 edited *Ritual and Remembrance: Responses to Death in Human Societies* (both Sheffield Academic Press) and wrote *The Christian Warrior in the Twentieth Century* (Mellen Press, in press). He has over the years written on *Municipal Capitalism (Local Government Studies*, 1987); *Asian Housing in Britain* (Social Affairs Unit, 1985); 'Duty and Self-sacrifice', in *The Loss of Virtue: Moral Confusion and Social Disorder in Britain and America* (Social Affairs Unit, 1993). He lectures mainly on the liturgies, theologies and sociologies of marriage and death.

Rabbi Dr Julian Jacobs has been Rabbi of Ealing Synagogue since 1989, and was previously Rabbi of Synagogues in Liverpool, Blackpool, Barking and Richmond. He has been the Member for Interfaith in the Chief Rabbi's cabinet since 1990, and is the author of *The Ship has a Captain: Judaism, Faith and Reason; From Week to Week: Bible Messages for Today;* and *Judaism Looks at Modern Issues.* He is married and has one daughter.

Revd John Kennedy is a Methodist Minister and Secretary of the Division of Social Responsibility of the Methodist Church. He was born in Clydebank in 1940. He was brought up in Swindon and served in the Royal Air Force as an electronics technician for eleven years. He studied theology at Richmond College in London and has worked on the South Coast of England, the

East Coast of Sri Lanka and in the East End of London. He has travelled in Central America and Western Europe, and currently works on British and European social issues. He is married with a grown-up son and daughter.

Rt Rev David Konstant has been the Roman Catholic Bishop of Leeds since 1985. He was ordained a priest for the Archdiocese of Westminster in 1954 and taught in schools for a number of years before being appointed as Religious Education Adviser for the diocese. He became an assistant bishop to Cardinal Hume in 1977, with special responsibility for the Central London area. Has served on various education bodies and is currently chairman of the Catholic Bishops' Conference Education Department.

Rev William F. Wallace is Convener of the Church of Scotland's Board of Social Responsibility. This is the largest voluntary social work agency in Scotland, with over 80 homes and centres, (including highly acclaimed work with confused elderly people and homeless people). The Board also reports to the Kirk's General Assembly on contemporary social, moral, and ethical issues. He was a Dental Surgeon before being called to the ordained ministry. He was educated at Glasgow and Edinburgh Universities and combined both trainings whilst in Ethiopia. As a Missionary Dentist, he was involved in treating and training throughout the country as well as ministering to a large inter-denominational congregation in Addis Abbaba. He is currently parish minister in Wick, Caithness. He has previously served as Convener of the Church of Scotland Community Care Committee and the Alcohol and Drugs Study Group. He is married with a son and three daughters.

Robert Whelan is the Manager of the Freedom and Responsibility Programme of the IEA's Health and Welfare Unit. He has written and produced a series of videos on social and medical issues including *The Truth About Aids, Facing Facts on Population* and *The Three Rs of Family Life*. He has written and spoken widely on issues relating to population and the environment, and his essay *Mounting Greenery* was published by the IEA's Education Unit.

Editor's Introduction

Robert Whelan

There appeared to be a widespread feeling at the end of 1993 that the conviction of two 11-year-old boys for the murder of two-year-old Jamie Bulger marked more than just another piece of shock-horror media hype. The revelation of the details of the capture, torture and murder of the infant, kidnapped in a busy shopping centre by two children who should have been at school, seemed to mark a new low point of wrongdoing. The Archbishop of Canterbury's response that 'This is actually a judgement on all of us in this country', albeit uncomfortably reminiscent of *Private Eye's* Rev. J.C. Flannel ('In a very real sense we are all to blame'), seemed valid. If children can murder children just for fun, what sort of a society have we created? Can we, the adult population, really feel that we are fulfilling our obligation as citizens to civilise and socialise the next generation, when we peer into the moral void which the stories of Jamie Bulger's killers seemed to reveal?

Although the two boys were judged by the court to be responsible for their actions, and were given custodial sentences, many still found it difficult to accept that mere children could have been wholly to blame for such deeds. There was a need for scapegoats, and Home Office Minister David Maclean turned on the churches. He accused the churches of failing to speak up on moral questions, and told a conference on juvenile justice that 'while the church spends its time discussing social issues, such as housing, politicians are left to talk about the importance of the difference between right and wrong'.[1]

Of course the condemnation of meddlesome priests by Conservative politicians was nothing new. Cynics suggested that there might be less objection to churchmen involving themselves in politics if they came in on the 'right' side of the debate. Others responded that some politicians had manifestly failed to set a good example by means of their own moral conduct.

It was in such an atmosphere of hostile debate that this little collection of essays was conceived. If it is true that large

1

numbers of young people are growing up unable to tell the difference between right and wrong, then the churches cannot absolve themselves of blame. On the other hand, as several of the contributors to this volume point out, it is unreasonable to expect the churches to keep the nation on the straight and narrow when only a minority of the population (estimated at 10 per cent) are churchgoers. Many who do not go to church still describe themselves as Christian—a majority of the population according to some polls—but, once again, churchmen will point out that it can make little difference to such people whether or not there is forthright moral teaching from the pulpit, as they are never there to hear it.

Whatever the percentage of the population which regards itself as nominally Christian, it would scarcely be accurate to describe contemporary Britain as a Christian society, given the very limited influence of the church over public life. To look to the church for a firm line on moral issues therefore raises the problem of how churchmen can be expected to imbue with moral absolutism people who do not share the faith from which the moral teaching is drawn. Religion is not just a set of rules but the manifestation of a living faith. Whilst it is possible to extract an impressive list of do's and don'ts from sacred texts, these are unlikely to appear compelling to those who do not accept the premise of belief on which they are based. One leading Parliamentarian who has been at the forefront of many campaigns on moral issues, particularly as they affect the family, makes no secret of the fact that he is not a Christian himself, but he believes that everyone should live by the Ten Commandments as they constitute a good set of ground rules. This may work for some people, but others would ask whence people are supposed to derive the motivation to control their impulses and desires without the conviction that comes from faith?

This is a question which often arises in connection with the involvement of the churches in education, and the teaching of religion in schools. To what extent, in a secular society, do we still expect schools to act as mission stations?

In November 1993, when the debate over moral education was at its height, Joan Bakewell used the Lothian European Lecture to address the subject of teaching morality. She noted that a recent opinion poll revealed that over 70 per cent of parents wanted their children to be taught that there is a God, but only 45 per cent wanted them to be taught that the bible is true.

She observed:

> There is obviously a hope that religious knowledge will put an end to crime, depravity and drug taking and motivate children to lead good wholesome lives ... These are false hopes.[2]

They are indeed if the religion which the children are taught is not related to faith. The naturally rebellious character of youth will hardly be tamed by a lukewarm exposition of the intellectual attractions of comparative religion, any more than a tendency to dangerous driving could be dealt with by presenting the Highway Code as optional.

The problem for Joan Bakewell and others is that, in a multicultural society, it is no longer acceptable to favour one set of religious beliefs over another. Christian apologists object that if they cannot maintain, even in church schools, the claims to exclusivity of Christianity, then their hands are tied. How can the church be a motor of moral instruction when the clutch is being held down to disconnect it from the engine of faith?

There are differing views on the desirability of a multicultural society. Is it a blessing, a mixed blessing, or not a blessing at all? There are also disagreements as to whether multi-culturalism really implies holding to your own beliefs while respecting those of others, or giving up on belief altogether. What does not seem to be in dispute, however, is that there was a time, within living memory, when there was more certainty about moral values in society than there is now. A generation ago parents could be reasonably certain that the values which they were trying to inculcate in their children at home would be re-enforced by the school, the church, the mass media and the judicial system. That consensus has, of course, completely vanished. Parents who hold what might be termed traditional views about the importance of honesty, hard work, and respect for persons and property may be shocked to learn that the promoters of Personal and Social Education in schools sometimes take a different view. They may be even more shocked, if and when they take their children to church, to hear moral relativism expounded from the pulpit. Finally, if their children should become involved with the law, they may feel that they are not helped in nipping a potential criminal career in the bud if children absorb the message from the criminal justice system that they can commit large numbers of crimes and get away with it.

It is not only parents who suffer from the fragmentation of the moral consensus. Teachers also complain that they are having to cope with the contradictory messages which children are receiving. Instead of co-operating with parents in the process of disciplining children, they find that some parents expect to hand over to the schools their unruly offspring and receive back well behaved paragons. As Dennis O'Keeffe said at a seminar held at the Institute of Economic Affairs, parents think they can be Dr Spock at home and leave it to the school to be Thomas Aquinas. There is also a widespread misunderstanding of what can be achieved through the schools. At a meeting held in the Institute of Education to launch Charles Murray's latest work on the underclass[3] a member of the audience suggested that classes should be organised for sixth form pupils to teach them how to be good parents. Panellist Norman Dennis responded that the attitude of any young person towards parenthood is the result of tens of thousands of observations of behaviour, coupled with expressions of approval or disapproval, which begin in infancy, and which inform the child of what is expected from parents. If the cumulative effect of these myriad stimuli has not inculcated a responsible attitude towards parenthood by the late teens, then it is dubious if a series of lessons, however inspired, can make good the deficit.

So what are the churches to do, operating on the ruins of a moral consensus and in a nation which is now largely unchurched? To what extent—if at all—are they to blame for the decline in standards of personal behaviour? This is the question which we have asked representatives of different faith traditions to address, and their responses constitute the remainder of this book.

Julian Jacobs has no doubt that the church must continue to exercise its prophetic ministry to the age, whether the message is popular or not. To neglect to do so is to share the guilt of the wrongdoer. David Konstant is equally forthright in his exposition of the Catholic Church's understanding of its mission to proclaim and teach moral principles. Michael Adie and William Wallace both argue that the church is a community of faith, not a set of rules, which promises the transformation of hearts and minds, and not just a list of rights and wrongs. John Kennedy advocates the teaching of a serious ethic of hedonism to meet the needs of an age which rejects both altruism and asceticism. Jon Davies calls for the state to return all schools to the churches or other voluntary associations, on the grounds that a state school system will never be able to teach moral values in the absence of any agreement about what they are.

After years of neglect, there has been a renewal of public debate about how the moral values necessary to a free and orderly society can best be transmitted to the next generation. Although the Institute of Economic Affairs holds no corporate views on any subject, we are pleased to present this third volume in the *Religion and Liberty* series as a contribution to this important debate.

Notes

1 Ford, R., 'Bulger case sparks row over morals', *The Times,* 26 November 1993.

2 An edited version of the speech was published the next day in *The Guardian*: Bakewell, J., 'Search for the secular soul', *The Guardian*, 26 November 1993.

3 Murray, C., *Underclass: The Crisis Deepens*, London: IEA Health and Welfare Unit, Choice in Welfare Series 20, 1994.

Re-sacralising Education and Re-criminalising Childhood: An Agenda for the Year 2132

Jon Davies

'CHILDREN: childrearing—see Parents'

This entry in the Index of the new Roman Catholic Catechism[1] is neither in that book, nor in any sensible understanding of the ways in which children learn morality, meant to imply that the task of childrearing devolves upon parents alone. Indeed, as the 'family' (it is now necessary to put this word into inverted commas: we should more properly talk about mere procreative practices) collapses or 're-structures' itself (so that for example parents should, for many children, now read parent), it may well be that it is upon the other agencies of child-rearing that greater calls will be made. Amongst these will be (obviously) schools and (perhaps not so obviously) the criminal justice system. In the past, such institutions complemented and reinforced the role of the monogamous nuclear family: *they assumed its existence as a viable entity*. As this type of family disappears, the business of rearing children—the 'community's' children—becomes more and more directly the concern of agencies of the state or of the community. Children are in effect being nationalised, paradoxically at the very time when the dominant political forces are privatising pretty well everything else: and it is in and from the non-family institutions of child-rearing that much will be expected. The radical nature of the changes which are upon us, willed or otherwise, can perhaps best be understood by a glance at the era from which, at some point in the early sixties, we made a most peculiarly rapid exit.

At the centre of the City of Newcastle upon Tyne stands a monument to Earl Grey, the British parliamentarian who in 1832, after thirty four years in the attempt, successfully piloted through Parliament the first of the Representation of the People Acts which (purposefully or not) created the electoral basis of

British Parliamentary democracy. The monument was erected in the early 1830s. On the *front* of the plinth on which the monument stands are inscribed the usual laudatory words which commemorate such accomplishments. The really interesting words are, however, to be found on the *reverse* side of the plinth. Here, in 1932, the City Fathers added the following quite extraordinary sentence:

> AFTER A CENTURY OF CIVIL PEACE THE PEOPLE
> RENEW THEIR GRATITUDE TO THE AUTHOR
> OF THE GREAT REFORM BILL.

The century of civil peace was 1832-1932. About which other country in the world would anyone in his or her right mind make such a statement? Is it, indeed, a credible thing to say about the United Kingdom, or were the monument re-dedicators of 1932 indulging in a large amount of moral smuggery, the reverse image of the moral panics which, allegedly, now attend so much of contemporary middle class comment? We do not really know, though it is clear from a reading of the press coverage of the occasion that great satisfaction was felt that the nation had coped very well indeed with the most turbulent social and economic changes and had emerged with its basic political and civilisatory structures intact and operable.

It is hard to believe that in the year 2032 a similar experience will enable our children or grandchildren to add a parallel inscription to the monument, commemorating the civilisation of the years 1932-2032. It is indeed much more likely that in that year our sons and daughters will censure the Earl for having so blithely set us on the road to democracy.

This may sound unduly pessimistic. There is, though, something terribly wrong with the world in which we live; and never has the Book of Revelation seemed to contain so much out and out realism. It may well be that we have to write off the century running up to 2032, and that we should concentrate instead on trying to lay down the beginnings of an archaeology of virtue for the century after that. I say archaeology to indicate that level of moral life in which certain values such as honesty or reliability or fidelity or loyalty are simply *taken for granted*, like the flatness of footpaths, or the oblongness of bricks, or the wetness of rain; the day to day unquestioned, ubiquitous attitudes and characteristics of day to day social living. We need to try to create a society in which it is abnormal and perverse to enweb one's home, inside and out, in intruder-detection devices (forget the fast dwindling memories of front doors that were never locked), or in which it is abnormal and perverse to ignore people in distress, as in these helpful tips for contemporary living provided by the Automobile Association:[2]

> Be careful when driving between 11.00 pm. and 5.00 am.
> If you see another driver in difficulty, drive on, and report it by telephone as soon as possible.
> Avoid stopping at isolated lay-bys.
> Don't stop if rammed.
> Don't accept help from strangers.
> Never pick up hitch-hikers.
> If all else fails, don't resist.

In a different, but related context, Detective Superintendent Kevin Orr, head of Strathclyde Drugs Squad, said: 'We have lost a large part of the current generation of young people to drugs. We can't abandon them, but we have to concentrate our efforts on the next generation'.[3] The task of laying down an archaeology of day to day virtue which can perhaps render such terrible advice and comments redundant will take many decades to accomplish—although, if the last forty years are any guide, such quotidianal virtues can be *destroyed* very quickly. If we are to move away from a welfare or dependency culture, broadly defined, we and our children and grandchildren will need something to move *to*, an *ideal* in terms of which our efforts are both guided and evaluated. As events in Eastern Europe seem to show, the sudden withdrawal of a welfare system can only too readily, in the absence of a virtuous alternative, lead to crime and parasitism, or worse, if restoring the market is simply seen as mere appetite unleashed. There will be specific versions of this problem in post-modern Western societies which try to reform the welfare system because the culture related to such a system has corrupted not only the recipients of public beneficence but also the largely middle class public sector which dispenses it. 'Back to basics', a very good and necessary idea, ran immediately into this problem of a decadent middle and upper-middle class from which, clearly enough, little moral leadership can be immediately expected. This is not simply a British problem. From the chilling statistic that America, with five per cent of the world's population, consumes fifty per cent of its illegal drugs, it becomes obvious that the welfare problem is not merely one of providing a set of sticks and carrots for the underclasses in their ghettoes, but of a suburban middle class which in its own behaviour now fails to set an example either to itself, or to the underclass, or indeed to the upper class. This is a problem the Victorians did not have, here or across the Atlantic.

I would like to discuss two things that need to be done to begin the slow task of rebuilding the moral bricks and mortar of our society. One, education must be re-sacralised; and two, childhood must be criminalised or re-criminalised. These two things are closely connected, in that the religious understanding of the way children become moral agents provides a better ground for social morality than does that understanding implicit in the current criminal law. Briefly, the law assumes that the child is a moral imbecile, and treats him or her accordingly: religion knows that the child is nothing of the sort—and takes him or her seriously.

Re-sacralising Education

In June 1994 the National Association of Head Teachers held their annual conference at Scarborough. The Conference had before it a survey of members which showed that eighty per cent of head teachers wanted the law on religious education in school changed, that seventy per cent could not hold a daily act of worship, that sixty per cent could not deliver the R.E. curriculum, and that thirty per cent said that they could not comply with the law on school assemblies and the teaching of the R.E. syllabus. Fifty per cent of the heads of *church* schools found the requirement of a daily act of Christian worship and the requirement to teach a broadly Christian R.E. unacceptable. The General Secretary of the Association, David Hart, along with his membership, sought the withdrawal of the policy which had led to fifty per cent of schools withdrawing from the teaching of R.E: and he accused the Secretary of State for Education, John Patten, of 'failing to recognise that the moral values could be taught outside the context of religious assemblies and R.E. lessons'.[4]

There has long been a history of teacher resistance to the presence, in schools, of an obligation to take part in acts of worship or to teach religion *as faith*, which in the United Kingdom means, or meant, Christianity. The 1944 Education Act required each local education authority to start each day with an act of worship. In those days, worship was simply assumed to be Christian worship, and because of this assumption was only minimally defined. For some decades after the War this may have been a reasonable assumption, but over the years the worship has tended to degenerate into a perfunctory, secular announcement session or Assembly. Increasingly, secularisation plus the arrival in Britain of large numbers of people of other faiths (Hinduism, Islam, etc.) led, not unreasonably, to the view that while religion *as religious studies* might well be a useful part of the syllabus, religion *as faith* would be inimical to proper education carried out by true professionals. Schools, that is, should not be mission stations, and as far as teaching religion in schools was concerned, this should take note of the fact that Britain was a multi-cultural society, in which no one religion should be given superordinate status.

Rather to the surprise of many, the Conservative Government after 1979 sought, in the Education Reform Act of 1988, to reinstate the act of collective worship *and* to provide for the compulsory teaching of R.E., in particular Christianity (described as 'the predominant religion in Great Britain'),[5] as part of the school curriculum. Head teachers were given an explicit duty to ensure that the act was carried out.[6] It was clear by the June 1994 AGM of the National Association of Head Teachers referred to above that the law was being most determinedly resisted and most comprehensively ignored. In its coverage of that AGM *The Independent* had as subheadlines 'Schools disobeying rules on religion' and 'Patten tells heads to obey law on religion'.[7] A 1993 Report by the Religious Education Council demonstrated how effective was the resistance of the teaching profession; the 1988 Act was being massively ignored. Even where there were qualified R.E. teachers on the staff of a particular school, they were being employed to do something else. Schools and local education authorities were masking their statistical returns in order to hide the extent to which they were breaking the law. Children between the ages of 14 and 16 spent less time on religious education than on any other subject other than music, and on average they spent about half an hour a week, this being less than fifty per cent of the Government's recommended minimum. The Report showed that not only were the majority of state-run schools failing to provide religious education for all pupils as the Act requires,[8] but that the situation in the 'opted-out' schools was almost the same.

The Report regarded its findings as 'an indictment of continuing inaction to combat under-provision by those centrally responsible',[9] i.e. it was critical of the role of *central* Government as the general funder of education and teacher training. It is also clear, however, that very large numbers of the teaching profession are adamantly opposed to the Act and to the principle of teaching R.E., either as 'Religion (any religion) as faith' or as Christianity. The British no longer go to Church in any large numbers and there is no reason to expect teachers to be any more religiously inclined than the generality of the population. Why, then, does Mr. Patten expect that his aims can be accomplished by relying on such a profession, deployed in the state system, and with a very different set of pedagogic and budgetary priorities? He would surely not wish to see a school appoint, as a teacher of zoology or botany, a person who thought that a banana was a kangaroo or, even more problematically, a person who thought that it was merely a matter of opinion, and a matter of but small importance, whether a banana was, or was not, a kangaroo. To ask a secular teaching establishment, embedded within a state school system, to teach religion or Christianity is a nonsense.

The only institution capable of teaching religion is a church. The only personnel capable of teaching religion are properly qualified (preferably ordained) practising members of the faith in question—Reverends, Rabbis, Imams. The only institution capable of teaching Christianity is a Christian church. Christian churches should teach religion in church schools. Every school should be a Sunday school. The very large sums of money currently being used in primary and secondary education should be steadily and determinedly transferred, via the existing opting-out procedures, to schools headed by an ordained Minister or committed believer. This would help the churches, fast becoming employers with more Ministers than parishioners, and would provide a surer long-term basis for a religious and moral culture than guitars in the aisles or televised songs of praise. Minority communities should have their own schools, run, as they undoubtedly would be, on religious lines. If an extensive opting-out procedure produced schools, teachers and school governors with a secular or humanist inclination, then fair enough. Sincerely held views are better than either cynicism or grudging compliance. The religious opted-out schools would, even if initially fewer in number, be a far better basis for a moral revival than the present idiocy of comprehensive, applied cynicism; and such religious, re-moralised, schools would very soon prove their worth and attract more and more pupils. With such competition and example, we might even get a better class of atheism.

Liturgy and the Law: Re-criminalising Childhood

The criminal justice system is not normally seen as playing a part in the socialisation and moral upbringing of a child: this is usually seen as the function of family and school. Yet it is the case that the rules of right and wrong upon which a society agrees are most explicitly expressed in its codes of criminal justice; and in court procedures and penal policy are to be found the mechanisms whereby a society expresses its attitude to those who break the rules. For many centuries there was a considerable overlap between these societal rules and the rules of good conduct of the church: what was sinful was also criminal, and what was criminal was also sinful.

Where the societal rules are expressed in the criminal law, and their exemplary proclamation in judicial and penal procedures, the rules about sin and its treatment are to be found in the liturgy of the church. The liturgy of nearly all Christian churches is very much more than a set of rules about how to behave in church. The liturgy provides a set of rituals and explicated precepts for all the stages of the life of the individual, inside and outside the church, seven days a week, fifty two weeks a year, all the years of his life. The liturgy provides a method of inculcating a sense of appropriate behaviour both of adults and of children and young persons en route to adulthood. In the Catholic Church, as the new Catechism has it, rites such as that of Baptism 'require a faith that is not a perfect and mature faith, but a beginning that is called to develop ... For all of the baptised, children or adults, faith must grow after Baptism'.[10] In this Catechism, as in some Church of England documents, the operating premise of this 'liturgy of maturation' is the intrinsically moral nature of the human, *qua* human, whether as child, young person, or adult. The liturgy creates no artificial divisions, by age or sex or race, within which the catechumen can be held to be free of the obligation to seek to behave morally, even (or even especially) while he or she is learning what that means. The liturgy assumes that a person can learn morality only when he or she realises from the start that he or she has a moral identity. The liturgy imposes upon the church, the faithful, the adults, an obligation to make precisely that assumption about its relationship to the catechumen. *The Revised Catechism of the Anglican Church* puts it this way:

> The Commission had been invited in its terms of reference to consider the production of two catechisms, one for children, one for adults. It decided in favour of a single catechism for young and old alike. For this reason, some of the questions and answers are beyond the immediate understanding of children. It is not, however, always a disadvantage to introduce a child to truths which he cannot fully grasp. Words and phrases which early became familiar may be drawn upon in later years to serve a more developed understanding.[11]

The Commissioners were in particular in favour of the catechetical form of learning, i.e. by question and answer, with the answer learned by heart or rote, because it 'emphasised the moral responsibility of the catechumen for his actions'.[12]

No one is here assuming that a child will fully understand at, say, age six, the full complexity of a moral lesson learned at that age; but no one doubts the necessity to begin to learn at that, or any other age, in order for the lesson to become part of the moral character of the adult that the child will become—and will become precisely because of what he or she learnt when young. As important as the learning, by heart, of the substantive teachings of the moral code, is the demonstrable experience of the insisted-upon obligation to try to learn. The fact that the community expects you to try to learn is probably more important than actual success, or failure, in doing so. The liturgy takes childhood seriously, as the time when the human being can, does, and should learn to be a moral being, aware of the fact that there is a difference between right and wrong, and that he or she has a duty to learn what that difference is. The fact that the youthful catechumen has not yet become an adult does not mean that he or she is not a moral being.

This rather labours the point. Any parent would tell you that child-rearing *without* such a respect for the integrity of a child would make parenting and child-rearing impossible! Such obvious truths did not however stop the Church of England in joining in the permissive rush to destroy the liturgical, and eminently practical, concept of the child as a moral being. Naturally, all this was done 'in the best interests of the child'. In its evidence to the Latey Committee on the Age of Majority The Church of England Board for Social Responsibility noted (i.e. claimed) that the idea of a minor was historically more to do with owning children as property than of protecting them while vulnerable. The Board felt that the time had now come to eradicate from the legal system all traces of the idea that the interests of the child should be affected by a consideration of anyone or anything other than the child himself, and went on to conclude that this desirable state of affairs would be arrived at by changing the law so that:

> (1) no child or young person is in any way restricted in his or her capacity or independence as a citizen solely for the benefit of any other person or persons and (2) that young persons should be protected, by legal incapacity to act independently, from having attributed to them legal responsibility likely to be unduly burdensome to a person of that age.[13]

In this formulation the Board of Social Responsibility (sic) abandons the human realism of its own liturgical tradition and elaborates the moral basis for the legal madness to which our criminal law has descended, i.e. that children and young persons are to be regarded as free of all relationships of responsibility with and to others, because these carry connotations of the 'ownership' of children which characterised the past (sic) AND, at the same time, they are, in their new found autonomy, to be free of any responsibility *which they themselves* find 'unduly burdensome'!

It is perhaps possible, on some perverse version of the doctrine of individualism, to subscribe to the notion of the legal autonomy of children, although it then becomes rather difficult to see why people would then have them or, having had them, remain long in their company.[14] More problematic, however, than the notion of the legal autonomy of children, is the second proposition advanced by the Board of Social Responsibility, i.e. that such legally autonomous child-persons should then, in the full possession of their individuality, be free of any responsibility for what they do! Such an outcome would appear to be palatable only to the most unctuous of the many varieties of unctuous theologies and philosophies produced in this half century.

Yet it is down this path that our criminal law has gone. In the United Kingdom child-persons under the age of 18 commit the vast bulk of crime—and a vast and growing bulk it is. Yet until they are ten years old, these persons are assumed to be incapable of knowing, *and therefore free from having to make any effort to know*, the difference between right and wrong, the difference between what is lawful and what is not. There is, to use the legal term, an 'irrebuttable presumption' that they are moral nullities. From 10 to 14, there is a 'rebuttable presumption' that they are so constituted, i.e. a prosecuting lawyer can seek to prove that the child or young person was indeed able to know the difference between right and wrong, between the legal and the illegal. From 14-18, when as young persons they are assumed to have acquired a capacity to know right from wrong (how?), and to therefore be available and amenable to criminal proceedings, even so they are in fact treated very differently from adults, a legal status they attain fully only after 18.

For most purposes, the pre-18 age group is effectively beyond the reach of the law; yet at the same time it is responsible, directly and indirectly, for the bulk of crime.

No increase in the numbers of police, or in the number of places available at custodial establishments, will be of any use whatsoever unless this legal immunity is removed. We must criminalise, or re-criminalise, childhood. Changes in the law which were announced at the time of writing do not deal with the basic fallacy of the law as it relates to minors. The proposed changes increase the range of offences for which people between the ages of 10 and 14 (to whom the principle of 'rebuttable presumption' applies) may be tried. This alteration, by reforming, merely re-enforces the error. The error is to locate societal response to an offence in the *age* of the putative offender. What possible difference does it make to the victim of a crime, or to the community, if the victimiser is eight or thirteen or thirty, any more than if the victimiser is black or white, male or female? The law, that is to say the police, should at the moment of arrest be concerned solely with the agency of the offence, not the age or colour or sex, or anything else, of the putative agent. An act either is, or is not, a crime. If it is, the perpetrator should be identified as a criminal, a person breaking the rules which other people abide by and without which no community can persist, never mind flourish. There should be an irrebuttable presumption that every human being is a moral human being, capable of knowing right from wrong. That principle, clearly established, and seen as a rule for life for all, may begin to restore our moral culture.

This does not mean that the sea will be full of ship-loads of little babies, toddlers and teenagers being sent, somewhat late in the day, to the colonies. It means that the criminal justice system, seen as one of the institutions necessary for the propagation and inculcation of moral values, will be seen to be doing its job in a way in which it is not at present. Indeed, at the moment the criminal justice system is propagating amorality. The ordinary reader may be unfamiliar with the concepts of irrebuttable and rebuttable presumption: the objects of such legalities, the actual or potential juvenile delinquents, are only too familiar with them. *They* know that if, out of a large gang, an under-10 offers himself as the agent of whatever it is they are up to, then the police are helpless. *They* know that any apprehension of such a juvenile is more likely to get the constable than the juvenile into trouble. *They* know, that is, how feeble the law is and how free of restraint they are. *They* know that they can behave as moral imbeciles, and many of them do so. They are free to maraud around in their neighbourhoods, the objects of fear to most, the objects of admiration and emulation to too many others. The criminal justice system proclaims their invulnerability, not their immorality. The young are a No Go area.

The Monument in 2132

A free society can be free neither of values nor of proper institutions for inculcating them. Historically, four mutually interdependent and mutually supportive institutions—the family, the church, the school, the law—have been the major institutions overseeing the socialisation of the young. They have all gone their separate ways—the family into confusion and schism, the church into dogmatic liberalism and minority status, the school into amoral secularism and po-faced sociology, the law to the moon. It may seem paradoxical that I should be seeking from a church which so resolutely relativises its own teachings a source of moral leadership in the years ahead. Perhaps the General Secretary of the National Association of Head Teachers was correct in asserting that moral values can be taught and learnt without involving religion. Perhaps—but equally, no doubt, one could read Shakespeare in the Swahili language. Why make things difficult? Our moral discourses are still, if dimly and recedingly, located in the language of the Christian religion, and a renaissance of such discourses is more economically to be elicited in a re-energising of *that* language, rather than in seeking to import another one. And it is perhaps possible that the English church lost its way, or it losing its way, not so much because it is losing congregations and closing churches, but because it has lost its schools and surrenders its responsibility for the moral education of the young to a flaccid and deluded juvenile justice system and a secular and amoral state school system. In re-invigorated, re-sacralised schools, and in a re-humanised criminal justice system, teaching and practising the logic and hopefully the substance of long-established 'liturgies for living', we *may* find the reversal of several post-war decades of cheerfully volunteered-for corruption, which has infantilised our nation. I stress may: there is certainly no guarantee, either in my modest suggestions, or in larger schemes, that the future is alterable. It may well be that in the year 2132 our descendants will see the monument in Newcastle upon Tyne as presiding over nothing more impressive than a gigantic crime-filled crèche called Great Britain.

This chapter is based on a talk given at a conference sponsored by the National Review Institute.

Notes

1 *Catechism of the Catholic Church*, London: Geoffrey Chapman, 1994.

2 *The Guardian*, 23 October 1993.

3 *The Independent*, 9 June 1994.

4 *The Independent*, 3 June 1994.

5 *Religious Education and Collective Worship*, London: Department for Education, Circular 1/94, 1994.

6 Education Reform Act, London: Department for Education, 1988, s.10(1)(b).

7 *The Independent*, 1 June and 3 June 1994.

8 Education Reform Act, London: Department for Education, 1988, s.2(1)(a).

9 Religious Education Council of England and Wales, *Time for Religious Education and Teachers to Match: A Digest of Under-Provision*, Lancaster: St. Martin's College, p. 1.

10 *Op. cit.*, p. 284.

11 *Archbishops' Commission to Revise the Church Catechism*, Church of England, 1962, 1992 edition, p. iii.

12 *Ibid.*

13 *Latey Committee on the Age of Majority*, Cmnd.3342, July 1967, pp. 53-4.

14 For a more extended discussion of the effect of such attitudes to childhood see: Davies, J. (ed.), *The Family: Is It Just Another Lifestyle Choice?*, London: Institute of Economic Affairs, Health and Welfare Unit, 1993.

Why is the Church so Bad at Making us Good?

Revd John Kennedy

As a keen young Methodist, more than thirty years ago, I remember looking up the hill and wondering what Lincoln Cathedral was for. I wasn't a complete Philistine. I loved both the Alhambra and Toledo Cathedral. But I knew they were historical relics of an official religious order in which I had no part.

Recently I looked down the hill at Durham Cathedral, and began to wonder again, but this time less patiently. Official religion retains an expensive, prestigious and ineffectual location in British society, and at a time when the whole nation feels immersed in moral catastrophe. The Churches are isolated in an official role which prevents them from being distinctively Christian, and inhibits the theological imagination which ought to nourish their life. It is the Church of England that mainly suffers this isolation, but so do the Roman Catholic Church and the Church of Scotland; it is only circumstances that deliver the Methodists from similar pretensions.

The End of Asceticism

There are powerful reasons why the Church cannot fulfil the role of External Examiner that society seems to require of it. It takes some moral courage to resist this demand; every time a terrible event throws us into a slough of shock and grief, the pressure grows to force the Church to make us better. There is, however, a quite different model of morality which society ought to pursue. And there is a rather different morality that a liberated Christianity can both teach and learn from. It will take a great deal of bravery for the Church to acknowledge this.

It is time to recognise that the Church is enmeshed in a moral tradition which is ascetic and altruistic, and which has been shaped by the centuries in which celibacy was celebrated

19

as a high virtue. By contrast, contemporary society is modelled
by a desire to fulfil its appetites and to further its interests,
accepting more or less responsible constraints on its self-seeking
behaviour. Its values are essentially hedonistic. There has been
a tendency to pretend that our society suffers from a failure of
an ascetic ethic, whereas in fact we suffer from the failure to
recognise, develop and practise a proper hedonism. Our society
rather urgently needs to conduct an open exploration of what it
is we live by, as private, intimate and political beings; that is,
we need to develop a public ethic. Such an approach needs to
come to terms with our actual, real-life behaviour. We are still
at the stage of seeking to be honest about what we are up to.

There are three areas in which the Church seriously inhibits
this kind of ethical development. First, **Christian belief**. It is
fine that a large minority of the population shares Christian
belief. It is also quite acceptable that there should be disagreements in matters of faith between, say, Anglicans, Catholics and
Pentecostalists. But it is confusing when successive Bishops of
Durham disagree so sharply on a matter as central as that of
the resurrection, when each has an official role in an official
Church. Successive governors of the Bank of England tend to
have less interestingly divergent views on the nature of money.
The more adventurous may regret this; the public at large is
glad to be spared the confusion.

The issue becomes sharper when theology connects more
directly with ethical concern. The debate on the nature of Hell
has recently reopened. This is the theological equivalent of the
traditional Commons debate on capital punishment; indeed the
political and theological debates are uncomfortably similar. But
surely such a debate ought to have some consequences for a
public ethic, and ought to have some kind of outcome. Are the
agreed sanctions on personal behaviour external, or internal, or
eternal—or what? We can extend debate indefinitely on this and
many other subjects, but not if our theological meanderings
divert us from the development of a public ethic.

Second, the question of **Christian practice**. Our ascetic
tradition forces us to apologise for our appetites and interests
rather than to be responsible for them; the Church can't think
straight about sex and money in a society where they are rather
important. It does, for instance, seem truly odd to spend time
discussing the sexual behaviour of the heir to the throne. It
seems almost compulsory for the Prince of Wales to be regarded

as chaste, but does this go for the rest of us? A public ethic may well rest on such a foundation of elaborate and sophisticated pretence, provided that this is what is desired, rather than merely endured. Appetite must be legitimised before it can be civilised. Again, an antique system of belief gets in the way of proper ethical debate.

So, too, with money. Christendom has engendered endlessly ingenious ways to make money, and then to be apologetic about it: 'gelt and guilt aye gang thegither'. It is clear that the official Christian ascetic and altruistic tradition cost a lot to set up and quite a lot to maintain, and that there is not much left over for the actual practice of altruism. Nonetheless, the tradition is set firmly in a context of self-denial and self-giving that sits oddly with the way that most people actually live. In contrast, it is encouraging to see how the Labour Party has sought to legitimise interest, with a view to civilising it. A further contrast lies in the way that this formidable task has been furthered by a striking alliance of Christians at the top of the Party, largely without benefit of clergy.

Third, and most difficult of all, is the question of **authority**. On the one hand is the real life of the Church. A community numbered in millions contains much idealism and human frailty, posturing nonsense and hard-won experience. It is richly diverse. But the official voice of such a body is forced to sound oddly inappropriate. It can hardly be heard unless it speaks *ex cathedra*—a disembodied voice, emanating from a great height. And if it is diffident about speaking with such authority, the silence is naturally much complained of. It is important to recognise the difficulty that the Church has when it is no longer a plausible referee, but has not yet learned how to be an effective player.

This account of the official Church in search of a public ethic lacks, to put it mildly, theological precision. But cool, footnoted detachment makes the connection between Christian theology and a public ethic obscure to the public. To the faithful, of course, it is not like this at all. We feel ourselves held by the grace of God in ways that literally defy description. Yet we have to make sense of the self-giving love of God in such a fashion that we can understand why we behave in one way rather than another. Making the connections between theology and ethics is a subtle, demanding and fulfilling activity—for the Christian. But this activity has been vitiated for generations by the wish to be responsible, in a somewhat grandly imperial way, for the morals of society at large. It is that empire whose ruins we now gaze upon, and whose ascetic and altruistic monuments loom over us so oddly.

Fun with Sex and Money

In the meantime, and by default, we behave as a society in all the ways that cause such concern. And it seems about time for us to come clean, to seek to develop a thoroughgoing hedonism, to replace a half-hearted and failed ascetic-altruistic morality. This attempt may sound simply indulgent and self-serving, easily caricatured as 'fun with sex and money'. But there is much more at stake than this; indeed, some will see such an approach to ethical development as an attempted renewal of the classical, pre-Christian exploration of the bounds of hedonistic practice. Others will feel they stand in the tradition of Tom Paine, Adam Smith and George Eliot. It soon becomes necessary to talk about *serious* fun with sex and money (and to reflect that fun with Adam Smith and George Eliot would be much too serious for most of us).

A serious hedonistic ethic has to take seriously the questions of belief, practice and authority, but moves the ground of the argument.

First, **belief**. A hedonistic ethic can frankly acknowledge our private appetites and material interests: it is, in fact, serious about sex and money. Such a moral community can also be serious about creating an agreeable society. It can have sympathy for those who suffer the ills of society, and can imagine how it might be different. But such an imagined society employs an ethic of **mutual obligation** so far as possible, rather than one of altruism; it is concerned to share the enjoyment of appetites and the pursuit of interests.

Such an ethic may also find fulfilment in the deferment of immediate gratification; it is possible to want clean air more than another car, to adopt rather than to invoke the technology of reproduction, to want to feed Somalia or free Bosnia. But when such an impulse arises out of a sense of the value of mutual obligation, rather than unconditional altruism, it is likely to be better at feeding and liberating. Serious fun demands serious choices.

Second, **practice**. An ascetic, altruistic critic will be sceptical of hedonism in practice—surely anybody can have fun. But consider marriage. The Christian tradition of marriage is the classic expression of the ascetic-altruistic ethic. Yet it is quite likely that a partnership unashamedly designed to raise children and to acquire property will thrive as well as one founded on a commitment to a mystic eternal union, wreathed in the illusions of romantic love. Likewise work. Many of us work to help others, and we are often reasonably rewarded for doing that. We, in turn, are helped by others who are similarly rewarded. In short, we work within a context of mutual obligation. Such professional commitment to a humane society need not be inferior in outcome to one fed by altruism; indeed, a lack of overheating self-righteousness may be a positive advantage. So it is quite conceivable that the actual outcomes of a hedonistic public ethic can be recognised as desirable even in ascetic-altruistic terms.

Third, **authority**. An authoritative hedonistic ethic seems a contradiction in terms, but only to the naïve. Many would argue that modern commercial consumerism is just the kind of hell in which people are compelled to enjoy, but only the compulsion is real, while the fun is illusory. Brave hedonists should test the authority of their creed where modern society works least well, like a tough estate in East London. Any attempt to establish a fulfilling life in such a setting strikes immediately on the brutal, deep-down unfairness suffered by such a community. Indeed, it is this unfairness that stops the mouths of so many inner city teachers: they can't deploy a useful morality with much conviction when life around is so desperately immoral. A serious hedonist should be prepared to pay what it costs to help people become healthy, and employable, and better able to live together in families and neighbourhoods.

Such a vision is driven by the desire that all should be empowered to fulfil mutual obligations. Such hedonists would abandon the grim pursuit of equality for its own sake, that vengeful child of the ascetic-altruistic tradition. But they would have hard things to say about a trivial and vicious commercial culture which compels people to consume rather than to enjoy one another.

So a hedonistic ethic would give voice to the unfairness that makes the enjoyment of appetite and the pursuit of interest so perverted and diminished; but it would tend to pursue actual enjoyment rather than abstract justice. The project's prospects of success are certainly better than those of an official religious tradition that deals so gingerly with human devices and desires.

Every day brings us fresh illustrations of the need for a public ethic that can take the rough and the tumble of contemporary real life. For instance, many teachers in the setting that I describe are extremely unhappy about enforcing the kind of religious practice and instruction that the Department of Education currently proposes. It is also clear that we cannot cope with the real problems of sexuality in a hedonistic culture without being explicit in a fairly hair-raising way about what people do, and imagine doing, with one another. So we are compelled to talk about sex, in public, with children, in ways that would quite recently have been incredible. Some of us still cannot cope with the notion that this is what a school nurse is actually hired to do, and may even do as part of her Christian vocation. Many of us long for the days when it was credible to manage a less overtly hedonistic society according to ascetic precepts, but it is no longer possible!

What is proposed here is a frank attempt to give moral content to civil society—indeed, to help develop a workable public ethic that fosters civility in society. Unfortunately, we have not let ourselves experiment with the creation of an honest contemporary ethic. And one of the chief blocks to this enterprise is the status that we sometimes seem compelled to give to Religious Education—the propagation of an ascetic, altruistic morality in a world struggling to be responsibly hedonistic.

A Radical Alternative to Hedonism

There is an important place for the Christian community in the pursuit of a modern morality—arguably a place given by God. Our kind of hedonistic world struggles to shape its own integrity. There are all kinds of Christian responses to that struggle. One Christian response seems particularly attractive. It stands in considerable contrast to secular belief, practice and authority. In such a Christian context there is a commitment to obedience, but this is a constraint so graciously experienced that it counts as freedom. Here it is God, not the world, that is enjoyed. Here God's unconditional love shown in Christ is experienced so intensely that the prudential world appears a pallid thing. And this world view is shared in the experience of worship, fellowship, common discipleship.

This way is heroic, intense, and essentially sectarian, though not necessarily exclusive or judgemental. The followers of this way are able to recognise the difference between a serious hedonistic commitment and simple self-indulgence; but they are clear that their kind of Christian ethic has a quite different logic and integrity.

In short, an ardent Christian way of experiencing and sharing life cannot conceivably be deployed as an agreed public ethic. This is the fatal flaw in any attempt to use public education as a means of inculcating ethical behaviour on the basis of Christian theology. When the Secretary of State for Education appoints himself as a latter-day Savonarola, we have descended into absurdity. But it is an absurdity which has its roots in the public wish that the Church should teach us how to be good. It is far better that society should shape an agreed public ethic which springs from its own needs, acknowledging a common debt to the Christian tradition and a common humanity with Christian believers, but not making each other prisoners of beliefs we do not share.

Getting on with the Job

Rt Rev Michael Adie, Bishop of Guildford

The murder of James Bulger in 1993 by two ten year old boys, one of whom was at a Church of England school, raised sharply the questions: Has society lost its way? Has the church failed society as a whole, and children in particular?

Every generation judges that things are not what they used to be, and fears we are travelling downhill, so it might be argued that the Bulger murder was just another milestone, marking undoubtedly a deep personal tragedy, but in more general terms registering little more than one more mile along the social road. There is in fact persistent debate about whether there is more violence and vandalism than there was, and maybe we shall have to wait longer for history to make a reliable decision. Perhaps what is new is our recognition that, however we compare with the past, we are a violent society, and violence is combined with a scepticism about authority. All institutions—monarchy, parliament, politicians, police, the judicial system, the church—are questioned in our age of cynicism. This cynicism means that anyone or any institution which teaches with a claimed authority about right and wrong is challenged and approached with scepticism.

The church cannot hide behind that cynicism, nor can it escape blame. If society has lost its way then the church stands indicted—and for one basic reason: one third of the schools in our national education system are provided by the churches, and over a quarter of the teachers being trained are in church provided colleges. If schools and teachers have failed, then so have the churches. But before we blame teachers and the churches it is worth identifying some confusions in the way of making any assessment of what the churches might have done or should be doing.

First there is an assumption that teaching young people about right and wrong will secure the status quo, and undergird society as we knew it. The government seemed to assume this in its White Paper, *Choice and Diversity*.[1] In pressing the need for moral values in education they included in their sample values respect for property and politeness. Such values have their place, but there are others of more significance, such as justice, integrity, compassion, forgiveness, truth. Once these values are taught and taken into the system, they may stimulate criticism of society rather than endorsement of it. That seems to have been the case in Africa where nearly all the first generation indigenous leaders were taught in mission schools and became social and ethical radicals. Teaching people about moral values and giving them the mental equipment for making moral judgements can disturb as much as reinforce the peace because morality involves both accepting a givenness about moral values and releasing our creativity.

A confusion also arises because some assume that we would benefit from a return to Victorian standards. We would then relearn thrift, respect for authority and responsibility for individual charity. Those are sound Victorian values, but it was the Victorians who also exploited children in the factories, disregarded human dignity in the new industrial slums, and turned a deaf ear to the cries of hunger in Ireland. There is not much to be gained from turning back to Victorian values, basic decency, or any other dream from some chosen period in the past. We undoubtedly inherit a valuable moral tradition from yesterday but we have to recreate it for today.

Another confusion is the assumption that morals primarily relate to individuals and only indirectly to social issues. In our age in which privatisation is prevalent, many have privatised religion and morality, regarding them as individual rather than social responsibilities, and matters of private opinion rather than social conviction. But even individual morality is not and cannot be clutched out of the air. We learn our morality through groups and societies which share common convictions. Part of the reason for any decline in individual morality is the erosion of the social conventions and common culture which endorse them. Social and individual morals are interlocking.

That brings us to the heart of the matter. All of us derive our moral standards from our beliefs or assumptions about what life is for. The Christian derives morals from his or her faith. The Christian moral code is not set in tablets of stone but stems from a living faith in a creator God who has transformed the mess of human life and leads us on to fulfilment.

Our belief is that this world, and the whole of humanity within it, is the work of God, who is like a potter moulding clay after his own image. The selfish streak in human beings is always resistant to those creative hands, but the potter works on. In the Judaeo-Christian tradition each individual is unique and of infinite value to the creator, and we cannot despise, ignore or jettison what he has made and given to us. In Christ God embodied himself in a human being and entered the world, transforming it from the inside, not condemning it from afar. Through his Spirit God is still moulding and trying to breathe life into his creation—not just human life, but divine Life. God is working to raise us to share his Life.

Christian morals are grounded in this faith. They treasure each individual, and do not condemn the less successful. We do not condemn and criticise others so much as work with them to transform them. We recognise that human beings are always reaching out and growing towards an unreached potential. So the Christian moral code is not just applying an ancient and static set of moral laws: it is dynamic and creative. The Christian moral code is not a law which we are bidden to obey and are assured of punishment if we fail to keep it, but a statement of human potential. If we wish to attain to the fullness of human life, then here are patterns and standards which will set us free to do just that. Christian moral codes are not minimum standards but guides to our true potential. The Archbishop of York, discussing the morality of human rights, raises our sights:

> There is a dynamic in human rights language which goes beyond the assertion of some general principle, some rational conclusion, and actually grasps hold of new possibilities. Maybe we are not talking about something inherent in human nature at all, but about something human beings can aspire to, create, discover, will, work towards, precisely because human nature is not fixed, static, given once and for all, but open-ended, always capable of further growth, full of further potential.[2]

It is perhaps significant that this fine statement of our human potential comes in a consideration of a comparatively recent moral development—human rights.

If this is an approximate description of the nature of Christian morality then we see that it is both accepting a tradition from the past and being creative in response to a living God. Christian morality is related to what people of other faiths and none understand to be the purpose of human life and the nature of humanity, but also draws on particular beliefs.

Over the past fifty years there has been in our society a drift away from a commonly held Christian belief. In some small part this maybe due to the growth of other religions. Some of them in fact share many of the same human values and moral standards that Christians hold. The major reason for the formal abandonment of Christian values has probably been the mistaken belief that now we have science we no longer need the hypothesis of God, and everything has to be verifiable if we are to accept it. Science and philosophy have moved on from such assumptions and both are now more accommodating of the metaphysical and the spiritual. Meanwhile the damage has been done. Many teachers, still unaware of more recent developments in science and philosophy, are cautious about Christian belief and not always sure of the grounds of our morality.

Another factor in the situation has been the suspicion that if anyone teaches Christian moral standards he or she is trying to make converts. We need to say again and again that schools are for education, not for proselytising, and the classroom is for teaching, not converting. Sensitive to this criticism, too many teachers have been hesitant to reveal their own convictions, while others have taught with such detachment that it has reinforced the assumption that morality is a private affair and each person's opinion is as good as that of his or her neighbour. We need more people teaching with enthusiasm and passion but also encouraging analysis and criticism. Young people undoubtedly need moral guidelines, but they also want to argue out *why* some things are right and others wrong. They deserve spirited teaching which engages with their moral dilemmas rather than with those of their parents. They deserve to be introduced to inherited values and standards and encouraged to enter them, challenge them and make them their own, perhaps changing some of them in the process.

Teachers are often blamed for failures of society. When people do not behave as we want them to, we ask why the teachers haven't taught them right and wrong. But when society has largely ignored the Christian faith from which morals are derived, when public figures do not adhere to such moral standards as we used to accept, it is no surprise that teachers and the churches cannot put right what society as a whole has got wrong.

Courageous efforts are being made by the churches through their schools to promote sound moral thinking. Aided church schools have adhered courageously to their trust deeds. They have sustained their Christian ethos, ensuring through the whole style of the school and hidden curriculum the Christian moral standards that are made explicit in the context of R.E. But when parents are indifferent or unsupportive, where society has ignored the issues, the school alone can achieve only limited results.

The churches press on quietly with their undergirding of moral values in their schools, in their pulpits, and in their diverse activities. Much of their teaching is informal, practical and unsung. In County Durham, for instance, the West Pelton Outdoor Activity Centre was formed eleven years ago by the church in partnership with the Probation and Social Services. This centre provides the outdoor activity element where Christian people can work alongside people who have been referred by alcohol and drug dependency units and with prisoners on temporary release. This is not a scheme for proclaiming moral standards from a distance, but working them out alongside people who have failed. Another example of what the church is doing is the Young Mothers Peer Education Project in Great Yarmouth. The church works with other agencies to enable young single mothers to go into schools and clubs to explain to their peers the social and human costs of teenage parenthood. Again, this is not telling people how to behave but working alongside them to hammer out a morality which makes sense and appeals.

Such projects may be small-scale but they are indications of how the church engages with people who know they have run into moral difficulties and struggles with them to make moral sense of damaged lives. Such small-scale work may well be more effective than well-publicised formal programmes and moral lectures.

The churches are not beyond criticism in their work to improve moral standards but they are not as inept as much superficial criticism implies. We are getting on with the job without diverting too much time to promotional publicity.

Notes

1   *Choice and Diversity: A New Framework for Schools*, Department for Education and the Welsh Office, Cmnd.2021, 1992, 1.30.

2   Habgood, J., Archbishop of York, *Making Sense*, London: SPCK, 1993, p. 106.

Who is responsible? A voice from the Jewish tradition

Rabbi Dr Julian Jacobs

Perceptions are important. If only a section of the public feels that the churches have failed then, even if those perceptions are wrong, it becomes necessary for religious leaders to speak out more clearly, more forcefully and more unequivocally against the present-day evils which engulf our society. The possible claim by some that they will not be listened to, and indeed that they will only make matters worse by antagonising others, is not a valid one. One thinks of the denunciations of the Hebrew prophets against the social and moral evils of their day. Those prophets, especially Jeremiah who is a tragic figure, were lonely heroes who incurred the opprobrium and even the ridicule of their opponents for their stand, and yet today, many centuries after they first proclaimed their message, their words are still valid and still speak to us in eternal tones. To swim against the tide is not easy, but in the end truth prevails.

There are a number of reasons why it is important to speak out. Silence may be interpreted as acquiescence; one who keeps silent becomes a party to the wrongdoing. Moreover, it cannot be known with absolute certainty that a rebuke will be ineffective. A rebuke could possibly limit the wrong done to what has already taken place, halting the wrongdoer from moving further along the downward path. A rebuke also stops the perpetrator from blurring the distinctions between right and wrong by making excuses or rationalisations. And even if it does nothing else, a rebuke enables the protester to retain his own moral position and not be carried away by the tide himself. But one need not seek reasons for protesting against wrongdoing. To oppose evil is simply the right thing to do, and no further reason is required.

There is in the Book of Leviticus (5:1) a verse which states, 'If he does not utter it, then he shall bear his guilt'. The verse is spoken of one who possesses evidence but who fails to give testimony in a court of law when called upon to do so. It lends itself to a wider interpretation. 'If he will not tell he shall bear his guilt' in the sense that one who sees a wrong being committed has a duty to speak out and object. The spiritual leader has a duty to upbraid his followers even if he knows that his words will have no effect. The doctor has a duty to reproach the patient who is endangering his health even if he knows he will not change his behaviour; and the teacher has a duty to reprimand his recalcitrant pupil even if he is certain that his rebuke will fall on deaf ears. Only if they point out the wrong do leaders dissociate themselves from it, and only then can they be considered blameless.

To adopt a stern and forthright attitude is not to be taken as contrary to teachings about the spiritual values of compassion, repentance and forgiveness. These are clearly second best, however, and the ideal is not to do wrong in the first place. The easiest course, paradoxically, is to avoid the very first sin. It is hard to sin the first time. After that it becomes progressively easier. Those who avoid the first sin are truly blessed.

In this day and age religion must proclaim its message especially steadfastly because belief in the Creator of the universe and in His guidance of its affairs does not always have the powerful hold upon people that it had previously. This attenuation of the religious foundations of society may largely account for the low sexual and moral standards often found, instances of which occur virtually daily and which lead to the horrendous crimes of murder, violence and rape even against the elderly and children as never before. The message of religion is starkly simple: wrongdoing is against the will of God. There is a moral order in the universe, and neither the individual nor society can go against God's will and remain unscathed. Religious faith can be taught, and frequently it catches on. Of course, the message must be proclaimed in a manner that will not appear ridiculous to present-day listeners; there is no place for sermons on hell-fire and eternal damnation in the modern pulpit. However, although religious principles are the surest guide to right living, even the non-believer will accept the demands of morality because, on his premises, man alone is responsible for the way in which the world is run.

The religious person, while motivated by his religious faith and belief in God's guidance of the world, should also consider himself alone responsible for what he does and how he behaves. God has granted us freedom of the will, and our actions are in our own hands. To take a simple example, many people complain about the unacceptability of certain television programmes. Here, at least, one answer is patently obvious; they can turn the television off! The question, Have the churches failed? should not be understood to mean that the churches are responsible for the ills of society. Indeed, the very wording of the question could indicate an abdication of personal responsibility. In a modern democracy at least, the churches have no power to enforce their message; they can only pronounce it. Whether the message is heeded is up to each individual. Where children are under age parents are to be held responsible for what their children do, and where one is mentally incapable of taking responsibility that responsibility is transferred to others. In all other cases each individual is responsible for his own behaviour. The question should perhaps rather be worded, Have we failed the churches? The prophet Ezekiel, following Deuteronomy 24:16, uttered a powerful message about personal responsibility: 'The soul that sinneth *it* shall die' (Ezekiel 18:4, 20, emphasis added)—that soul, and not any other shall bear its guilt. When things go wrong children often exclaim 'It wasn't my fault!', but in real life people have to accept responsibility for their actions. The fault of the individual must be acknowledged. Until guilt is admitted there can be no incentive for change and improvement.

A basic guide for human behaviour was stated long ago in the Golden Rule of the Book of Leviticus: 'You shall love your neighbour as yourself' (Leviticus 19:18). However, because this command may appear too idealistic and impossible of fulfilment, the first-century Jewish sage Hillel worded it in the negative: 'Do not do to others what is hateful to you'. Here is a rule of thumb which can be understood and appreciated by everyone. It is the minimum requirement of ethical behaviour demanded of all human beings, linked to each other as they are by their common humanity.

Teaching Morality

Rt Rev David Konstant, Bishop of Leeds

Teaching what is right and wrong is the duty of every individual and of society. It is a responsibility that the Christian Church has accepted from the very beginning of its history and has implemented, both officially and more informally through its members. Underlying the first call to follow Christ was a call to conversion and repentance. In the New Testament letters there are clear indications about the relationship between faith and living, and instructions about moral living, in line both with the teaching of Jesus and with the constant tradition of the Hebrew scriptures. The official teaching of the Church, promulgated through its Councils, Papal letters, and other authoritative statements has continued this instruction. Theologians from St Augustine onwards have explained and developed this teaching in manuals of moral theology, catechisms, and text books for students, while ordinary members of the Church have taken hold of this teaching for themselves so that the link between faith and living can be maintained and developed.

The Catholic Church has thus consistently and unambiguously accepted its responsibility to proclaim and teach what it believes to have been revealed by God, and what can be learnt by reflecting on human happiness and fulfilment. Inevitably, then, teaching about right and wrong presents itself under the double aspect of human fulfilment and command, obligation and law. The Church has always accepted and obeyed Paul's injunction to Timothy: 'preach the word, be urgent in season and out of season, convince, rebuke, and exhort, be unfailing in patience and in teaching' (2 Tim. 4:2). Such teaching is frequently criticised by others, either because it is seen as merely negative (the 'killjoy' syndrome), or because it is regarded as interference (the 'vestry' syndrome). The first criticism fails to recognise that although all law is a constraining influence, its proper effect is to bring greater human fulfilment to all; the second criticism fails to understand that human growth does not take place anywhere other than in society, and that it is there that people's personal and social needs can be addressed; and neither criticism acknowledges that the Church's overriding duty is to proclaim the truth as perceived to be revealed.

Knowledge of the Law

Knowing and understanding what the Law says is essential for living well. Jesus is quite clear: 'If you wish to enter into life, keep the commandments' (Matt. 19:17). He goes on to list the ten commandments; then he adds: 'You shall love the Lord your God with all your heart, and with all your soul, and with all your mind... And your neighbour as yourself' (Matt. 22:37, 39). Then later he says: 'A new commandment I give you, that you love one another as I have loved you' (Jn. 15:12). This is the love that is the basis of Christian moral behaviour.

The Law and Discernment

'Depart from evil, and do good; seek peace, and pursue it' says the Psalmist (Ps. 34:14). A clear invitation, though it somewhat begs the question. How does one tell what *is* actually right and *is* actually wrong? The original fall from grace is told as a temptation to discern the knowledge of good and evil and so to be like God: 'you will be like God, knowing good and evil' (Gen. 3:5). It is such an important and difficult matter that to be able to discern good and evil is seen as an almost angelic quality. King David is spoken of as 'like the angel of God, discerning good and evil' (2 Sam. 14:17), while Solomon's greatest gifts were 'wisdom, discernment, and breadth of understanding' (1 Kings 4:29).

However, law does not create the community's morality *ex nihilo*. It says do this or avoid that, but does not address the question of why precisely this or that is right or wrong, or why the law should be obeyed. In fact it is by reflecting on past experiences that the community begins to discern the difference between right and wrong, and is thus able to make law. Israel's experience of God's guidance and presence was part of the process by which the commandments—expressing and explicating the relationship of the members of the community to God and to one another—were first discerned. In such a process law-like principles gradually become clear; they can be applied to new situations and in turn the law itself may be clarified and developed. This process constitutes and flows from the com-

munity's life and can be called Tradition (with a capital T).
However, individuals in the community can never know all the
answers, nor can any one generation. No law can save us from
making fresh moral judgements because law can never detail the
infinite variety of human activities. Hence a moral tradition is
always developing further in its fresh understanding, and must
remain sensitive to the new experiences or the new situations of
each succeeding generation.

Moral Principles

Even though there will always be new situations not envisaged
by the law there are certain unchanging principles of right
action. These are universally, or almost universally, held. They
form the bedrock of all human moral actions; where people do
not accept principles of this sort there is social anarchy. Such
principles do not depend solely on a particular religious belief,
but arise also from a consideration of the conditions of human
growth and fulfilment.

Like all principles they are for the most part very general
statements. For example: 'Do good and avoid evil'—without such
a basic understanding the moral life is impossible; 'Do to others
as you would have them do to you'—the so-called Golden Rule;
'You may not do wrong in order to achieve something good'—the
end does not justify the means; 'Live not by lies' (the title of a
powerful article by Alexander Solzhenitsyn)—we are only truly
ourselves when we live according to the truth; 'Love and do
what you will'—a deceptively simple principle formulated by St
Augustine which focuses the essence of right action on
relationships.

It is often said that these are the laws written in the heart
of every person. Our teaching task, then, is not so much to
impart or impose them, as to enable them to become real and
personal principles of action. Those who make such principles the
basis of their personal choice are on the way to moral autonomy
and at the same time to fullness of life.

Conscience

Conscience is said to be a capacity for judging right and wrong.
More precisely it is the judgement that this, here and now, is
what we have to do. It is the primary means by which we grow
to a greater responsibility for our own actions. Obedience to my
conscience is the ultimate test of my moral integrity, so Cardinal

Newman could call conscience 'the aboriginal vicar of Christ'. It follows, then, particularly since conscience can be mistaken or ill-formed, that the education of my conscience is one of the most important aspects of my growth to maturity, and that such an education is lifelong. The habit of making the right moral choice is what defines the virtuous person, the person of integrity.

Our personal responsibility is to make moral decisions through the proper exercise of a well formed conscience. Such formation takes place through the influence of and personal reflection on the whole spectrum of our experience. This includes our inherited values (upbringing), our knowledge and understanding of law and history (instruction), the influence of others (personal relation-ships), the influence of society (including school, peer groups, the Church, the media—not all of which influences are necessarily for our good), an awareness of and a listening to God (prayer), the experience of making decisions both right and wrong (we can learn so much from this), and personal growth of every sort.

The Individual and Society

Growth to morality is a gradual discovery of our interrelation-ships with others and of our consequent obligations to them, particularly within the family, and also within the other communities to which we belong. Abstractly it is a movement from self-centredness and selfishness (which is an element of all wrongdoing) to an other centredness that paradoxically leads to a greater autonomy. Psychologically and sociologically it is discovering that we exist in society: we do and must live socially. That discovery begins in the family; socialisation and morality are two sides of the same coin.

In such growth we become increasingly aware that the rights of the individual are constrained by belonging to society. Society is more than the sum of individuals and depends for its health on the development of sound relationships among individuals and between individual members and the whole. 'No man is an island entire of itself'. The Sermon on the Mount speaks of the values and obligations of the Kingdom, where God reigns. Catholic tradition speaks of the common good as 'the sum total of social conditions which allow people, either as groups or as individuals, to reach their fulfilment more fully and easily. The whole human race is consequently involved with regard to the rights and obligations which result. Every group must take into account the needs and legitimate aspirations of every other group, and still more of the human family as a whole'.[1]

How the Church Teaches Morality

There are in particular four ways in which the Church teaches a way of life to its members, and proposes it to society as a whole. By proclamation, by education, by public debate, and particularly by example.

Proclamation: Occasionally the Church makes a public declaration about moral questions. This may be through a papal letter or other statement, or (very rarely) through a Council of the Church, the last of which was the Second Vatican Council (1962-1965). An important declaration made at that Council was *The Church in the Modern World*. This sets forth the relationship of the Church to the world and to all mankind, and examines in some detail certain aspects of life today in the light of Christ's teaching, such as marriage and the family, culture, economic and social life, the political community, the distribution of wealth, peace and war, and international relationships. In the thirty years since this was promulgated a number of Church documents have been written in which one or other of these aspects of life is treated in greater depth and detail. The corpus of teaching relating both to the individual and to society that has developed in this period is considerable.

Education: This is far wider than what is sometimes called nurture (the upbringing of children in the faith of the Church). It extends, rather, to the whole educational enterprise, since the Church sees all education as a seamless robe, each part of it exploring in its different way the one truth, which ultimately is God's unfolding of himself. This is why the Church consistently encourages and supports the provision of Catholic schools and colleges.

Within this enterprise religious education holds a privileged position. In all Catholic schools a substantial proportion of time is spent on educating their members to a knowledge and understanding of scripture, doctrine, liturgy and the Christian way of life. Recently a new Catechism of the Catholic Church[2] has been published worldwide. This is a substantial text which brings together what the Church teaches about the profession of faith (the Creed), the celebration of faith (the Sacraments), the life of faith (the commandments), and the prayer of the believer (the Lord's Prayer). It shows the proper harmony between faith and living. It will be a source book for new instructional texts for students of all ages for a number of years to come.

Public debate: The Church also teaches what she believes to be right and wrong by playing a forthright part in public debate. This is for all its members, both laity and clergy, to be involved in; even if they rarely influence the civil law they have the right and duty to make sure that what the Church believes and professes about matters of public moment is known and understood; they have a contribution to make to the common good. (The Catholic Church's stand on abortion and euthanasia, for example, is well-known.) Such matters should be debated openly, honestly and intelligently. If such opportunities are not available society is in great danger, and the failure of the Church to enter into such debate would be a failure of its duty to the world.

Example: This may be the most important way of all for the Church, both as an institution and through its individual members, to teach about the Christian way of life, remembering that if people are to listen to teachers it is because they live by what they teach. They are able to show in themselves the link between human fulfilment and a moral life. In a pluralist society, distrustful of authority, the Church needs to articulate its teaching about right and wrong in a way which is both deeply human and deeply rational: this is what will make its teaching persuasive. One reason people turned to Jesus was because his words and actions were in perfect harmony. He was a man of authority, with compassion for everyone; he listened, understood, encouraged, forgave, taught. The people trusted him, and they followed him through thick and thin, many of them even to their own martyrdom. The example of Jesus comes in the form of a command: 'Follow me ... If you love me keep my commandments ... Love one another as I have loved you'. The love demanded of his follower is the sacrificial love of complete obedience to the Father's will. It is from this that the meaning of the phrase, 'Love and do what you will', takes its particular power as the basis of all moral living.

In the first days of the Church its members shared all they had; 'they would sell their possessions and goods and distribute the proceeds to all, as any had need' (Acts 2:45). 'Look at these Christians' remarked an early writer, 'how they love one another'. Although this way of life did not last long, the value and need of such example remains.

The primary example is always that given within the family, often called the domestic church. This is where right and wrong are first taught, not by imposing rules, but by love and care. Family discipline depends on consistency, understanding, listening, firmness and gentleness, all within the framework of love and of Christian faith. This is the way in which children are led to moral autonomy.

We teach by what we are, rather than by what we say; it is when we are accepted as men and women of justice, truth and integrity, that what we say begins to ring true. It is when the Church is recognised as an institution of moral uprightness that its teaching on moral living becomes most effective.

Conclusion

In teaching a way of life to its members, and indeed to any others who may be able to hear such teaching, the Church fulfils a fundamental responsibility which it has accepted and exercised from the days of its foundation. It is not an easy task because the discernment of what is right and wrong is something deep and subtle, and has to begin anew with each new generation and each newly born person. Moreover in a society which tends to think of morality in terms of opinion, it is increasingly important for the Church to be able to show both the objective and rational nature of right and wrong and the call of the Christian Gospel. In doing this the Church is able to draw on its riches and so continue to proclaim the truth, to instruct, counsel, advise, encourage, chide, lead. This work of teaching a way of life is undertaken by all members of the Church—by parents, spouses, friends, clergy, teachers, catechists, bishops, and the Pope. All have duties and opportunities in this regard and, despite the many failures that all of us have to confess, for the most part discharge these responsibilities cheerfully and well.

Notes

1 *The Church in the Modern World*, Documents of the Second Vatican Council, 26.

2 *The Catechism of the Catholic Church*, Geoffrey Chapman, 1994.

Right and Wrong and Faith

Rev William F. Wallace

We are passing on to our children a society that is less civilised than the one we were born into. Knowledge has increased at an unprecedented rate but society has not improved. It is more self-centred. It is more violent. It is less honest. Personal relationships are less stable. There is a great sense of insecurity.

Recently there has been an outburst of national soul-searching about the state of the nation, with one group after another apportioning blame—to someone else, of course. The Church has had to take its share of criticism for failing to teach the rising generation the difference between right and wrong.

There is a sense in which the Church must always be prepared to accept responsibility when there is a decline in moral standards and social structures. No man is an island and the Church, as an important part of the community, cannot resort merely to saying the fault lies elsewhere. Jesus made it clear in the Sermon on the Mount that He expected his followers to be salt (preventing decay) and light (in the darkness).

But is anyone listening when the Church does speak? And when last did society really want to listen to the Church's message? In many ways the Church has never had a better time to expose the economic costs of society's retreat from Christian standards.

Dishonesty, whether it be shoplifting, insider dealing, tax evasion, or massive fraud, adds considerably to our everyday costs. AIDS, which is currently costing society an ever increasing amount in preventive health measures and research, could have been virtually stopped in its tracks by acceptance of traditional Christian morality of faithfulness within marriage and chastity outwith it. Addiction to alcohol and other drugs has social consequences for many families and financial consequences for most. Marriage break-down may help the legal profession through increased fees, but it swells the legal aid bill. The cost of treating offenders spirals ever upwards. And so it goes on. Maybe Christians are too slow to press home the true cost of the nation's turning from God.

Society hasn't been listening and, it can be argued, is paying a high cost for it. But is the Church speaking clearly enough?

Without being apologetic, the issues are not so simple as they seem at first sight. Take, for example, the matter of teaching right and wrong. It is one thing for the Church to know and to make clear statements on these issues—but who wants to hear? Does our society really want to know the difference between right and wrong? For a long time it has been railing at anyone who seemed to be 'negative'. However, the essence of making positive choices involves also having the moral courage to say 'No'. Does society want people with that type of moral courage? I can't believe that many people are really wanting to hear, for example, the seventh commandment, 'You shall not commit adultery'. I've had some pretty angry responses when I've preached on it inside the church—and inside a good solid Presbyterian church at that!

There is a further problem. Just supposing the message is really wanted, can we not identify with Paul when he said 'I have a desire to do what is good but I cannot carry it out' (Romans 7:18). People may want to do what is right and may wish they could say 'no', but how can they get the strength to do it? That gets us to the heart of a fundamental human problem. There is good in all of us but not enough strength to respond to conscience and swim against the prevailing consensus. People need to be radically changed and receive God's power before they can go God's way. They need to be re-born—and that is the rub. Proud twentieth century people are just as reluctant as first century people were to repent and cry to God for mercy and new hearts. The Good News of the Cross is still an offence to a largely self-centred society.

At the end of the day there are two sorts of people, those who are genuinely 'self-made' and those who are 'God's workmanship, created in Christ Jesus to do good works' (Eph. 2:10). I fear our society is still intent on 'D.I.Y.' solutions and is not yet ready to call for divine intervention.

People can talk about right and wrong. They may want their children to know what is right and wrong. They might even want a more moral society. But unless they want it so much that they are prepared to look beyond human solutions and let

God take over their lives and society there can be little prospect of change for the better.

This brings me to the final point. It is about what the Church has to offer our society. The Church is a community of people whose hallmark is faith in Jesus Christ. Faith is much more powerful and much more demanding than law. There is a simplicity of appeal about law (boundaries of right and wrong) that has a certain attraction to beleaguered people. It can stir a feeling that if only we do certain things and decry other things all will be well. Faith is much wider, much more stimulating, much more empowering than that. Faith involves trust in God. It involves acknowledgement that man and his society are not up to the tasks confronting them and that they need God's help. It involves accepting God's ways and God's standards, but it also involves the most exciting things that a human being can experience. It involves integration of body, mind and spirit. It involves the human mind being stirred by a Mind which is vastly superior, a Mind much more creative and more stimulating. It involves the experience of forgiveness and the removal of the burden of guilt. It involves a new sense of security through trusting God at all times. It involves receiving power from God. It is about receiving grace (unmerited favour).

To demand of the Church a list of rights and wrongs when all this is available is like asking for clear sign posts on a difficult track when the offer is to get you safely to the end of the road. It is like demanding a copy of the Highway Code when a Rolls-Royce is awaiting (with the Highway Code in the glove-compartment).

Faith offers so much more than a list of rights and wrongs. But what sort of appeal does it make to our self-satisfied, materialistic, hedonistic, technological age?

ORDER FORM—EVERYTHING HALF-PRICE

Title	Normal Price	Offer Price	Qty	£
Families Without Fatherhood (2nd Edition)	£7.95	£3.95		
Rising Crime and the Dismembered Family	£5.95	£2.95		
Reinventing Civil Society	£7.95	£3.95		
A Moral Basis for Liberty	£4.95	£2.45		
The Family: Just Another Lifestyle Choice?	£6.95	£3.45		
Equal Opportunities: A Feminist Fallacy	£6.95	£3.45		
Moral Foundations of Market Institutions	£7.95	£3.95		
The Emerging British Underclass	£5.95	£2.95		
Empowering the Parents	£6.95	£3.45		
Christian Capitalism or Christian Socialism?	£4.95	£2.45		
God and the Marketplace	£4.90	£2.45		
Medical Care: Is It a Consumer Good?	£3.95	£1.95		
Liberating Women From Modern Feminism	£6.95	£3.45		

Please add 50p P&P per book up to a

maximum of £2.00

Subtotal:

P&P:

Total:

✓

I enclose a cheque for £...................... payable to the Institute of Economic Affairs ☐

Please debit my Mastercard/Visa/Amex/Diner's card for £.................... ☐

Number: ....

Expiry Date: ....

Name: ....

Address: ....

....

....

*Please return to **IEA Health and Welfare Unit, Institute of Economic Affairs,***
2 Lord North Street, Westminster, London SW1P 3LB

ALSO AVAILABLE FOR HALF-PRICE

Liberating Women ... From Modern Feminism, Caroline Quest (Ed), Norman Barry, Mary Kenny, Patricia Morgan, Joan Kennedy Taylor, Glenn Wilson £6.95, 101pp, 1994, ISBN 0-255 36353-2

Caroline Quest argues that 'power feminism' ends up having as little relevance to most women as the 'victim feminism' it is directed against. It is, she says, 'for pre-maternal young women' and 'is of little relevance and help to the realities of life for the majority of real women'.

"It would be a mistake ... to take anything but seriously the essay "Double income, no kids: the case for a family wage" by the sociologist Patricia Morgan."

Margot Norman, *The Times*

The Moral Foundations of Market Institutions, John Gray, with Chandran Kukathas, Patrick Minford and Raymond Plant, £7.95, 142pp, Feb 1992, ISBN: 0-255 36271-4

Distinguished Oxford philosopher, John Gray, examines the moral legitimacy of the market economy. While upholding the value of the market economy he insists on the importance of an 'enabling' welfare state.

"one of the most intelligent and sophisticated contributions to modern conservative philosophy."
The Times

"This powerful tract ... maps out a plausible middle ground for political debate."
Financial Times

A Moral Basis For Liberty, Father Robert Sirico, commentaries by Lord Lawson of Blaby, William Oddie £4.95, 38pp, July 1994

Father Robert Sirico, a Roman Catholic priest and President of the Acton Institute defends the morality of liberty. His argument is criticised by former Chancellor of the Exchequer, Nigel Lawson, and William Oddie a regular columnist for *The Sunday Times*.

The Emerging British Underclass, Charles Murray with Frank Field MP, Joan Brown, Alan Walker and Nicholas Deakin £5.95, 82pp, May 1990

"Mr Murray... calls himself a visitor from a plague area, come to see if the disease is spreading."
Daily Telegraph

"Britain has a small but growing underclass of poor people cut off from the values of the rest of society and prone to violent, anti-social behaviour."
The Times